VALUES
OF THE
AFRICAN
AMERICAN
FAMILY:
THE KWANZAA CANONS

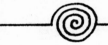

by JohnnieRenee Nelson

author of
POSITIVE PASSAGE:
EVERYDAY KWANZAA POEMS

Cover design by Judythe Sieck

ALSO BY JOHNNIERENEE NELSON

A QUEST FOR KWANZAA: POEMS $6.00

POSITIVE PASSAGE: EVERYDAY
KWANZAA POEMS $7.00

KUUMBA WORKS: 101 CREATIVE THINGS
TO DO AND MAKE FOR KWANZAA $6.00

KWANZAA LOVE $6.00

Californians: Please add Sales Tax.

Order from **House of Nia**   Shipping: Add
P.O. Box 151 $1.50 for first book
Bonita, CA 91902   and .75 for each
                              additional book.

To my Beloved Courtney

If the poet does not teach his song to the people, who will sing it?

-TANZANIAN proverb

NGUZO SABA

UMOJA   (Unity)
KUJICHAGULIA   (Self-determination)
UJIMA (Collective work and
   responsibility)
UJAMAA   (Cooperative   economics)
NIA   (Purpose)
KUUMBA   (Creativity)
IMANI   (Faith)

CONTENTS

CLARION CALL

CLARION CALL

African Americans - so called minorities
Are subjected daily to skewed priorities
Experience daily blatant indignities
All kinds of injustices, all kinds of obscenities
African American families strive to
resist them
By focusing daily upon their own value system.

Just imagine how phenomenal our community
would be
If we all practiced the seven principles
of Kwanzaa - unity,
Self-determination, collective work and
responsibility
Cooperative economics, purpose, creativity
And faith; seven values to guide us collectively
To a higher plane of spirituality
Values designated to nourish specifically,
The African American family.

Think about the impact
a Kwanzaa consciousness would make
If we were to internalize the Nguzo Saba
for " a minimum morality's sake"
Principles which reflect our own historical
foundation
Principles which promote cultural revitalization
If we are to have our community epitomized
Then the ways of our ancestors
must once again be emphasized.

The tree cannot stand up without its roots.
- ZAIREAN proverb

SHONA

Among the Shona
A family's success
Is weighed by their children's happiness
And the family's state of health
Not by the accumulation of material wealth.
Shona people sure are wise
To have the foresight to emphasize
Values that strengthen family ties
Traditions of sharing, traditions of caring
Traditions that instill dignity and pride
That generate beauty on the inside.

Among the Shona
The joy children bring
To the family union
Is the most valued thing
Along with the laughter that families share
And a respect and appreciation for others found
everywhere.
Shona people sure are wise
To have the foresight to emphasize
Values that strengthen family ties
Traditions of sharing, traditions of caring
Traditions that instill dignity and pride
That generate beauty on the inside
That generate beauty on the inside.

If you alone drink a medicine for long life, or to
stave off death you will be left alone in the wasteland.
-**ASHANTI** proverb

DRUM CALL

PRELUDE

First the drum call
Next the wazee enter
Then a candle is lit
The one in the center
The black candle which
Represents unity
On this first night of Kwanzaa
In the African American community.

A VISITATION OF SPIRITS

They come
They all come
The women with the hum
And the men with the drum.
Honored ancestors come who have
vanished from the earth
Children come too; those who have not yet
experienced birth.
The spirits of the yet unborn
and the long-ago-departed
Come so that the Kwanzaa festivities
can get started
For the celebration of Kwanzaa
is a spirited affair
With cultural fruits for all to share.

Ask the aged about good proverbs.
-**NIGERIAN** proverb

FAMILY REUNION

Just imagine what a great
Family reunion there would be
If we could celebrate Kwanzaa with
Our entire extended family
If we could communicate in Twi, Nguni, or Susu
Or perhaps in Yoruba, Sara or Zulu
If we could interact with those family members
whose ethnicity is Dan
Or meet our long-lost-cousins
the Ashanti? the Khoisan?
We could listen to the griots or
play mankala (an African game)
Or do something awesome
Like discover our "real" family name
Or perhaps just erect a pyramid
Like our Nubian ancestors did.

Wood may remain ten years in water but
it will never become a crocodile.
-LIBERIAN   proverb

<u>KWANZAA KARIBU</u> (Kwanzaa Welcome)

Habari gani?

Umoja, ujima or imani

Do you know the appropriate response to say?

It's the Kwanzaa principle for that day.

The first day it's umoja, then it's kujichagulia

The third day it's ujima, then ujamaa, then it's nia

The sixth day it's kuumba and the seventh day it's imani

These are the responses to the question "Habari gani?"

And when Kwanzaa has passed and it's just an ordinary day

"Njema" is the appropriate response for you to say.

If you know the beginning, the end will not trouble you. -East African proverb

PRAISESONG

Sing a song of praise
For each of the seven days
Kwanzaa is always
Celebrated on this soil
We'll begin this commemoration
With the pouring of the libation
A ritualized commendation
To our ancestors' toil.

ROLL CALL

DR. CHARLES DREW

SOJOURNER TRUTH

A. PHILLIP RANDOLPH

HARRIET TUBMAN

MAULANA KARENGA

IDA B. WELLS

THURGOOD MARSHALL

MARY McLEOD BETHUNE

MALCOLM X

DR. MAE JEMISON

CARTER G. WOODSON

INTERLUDE

While libation is poured
An ancestral roll call is enacted
a memorial to how our lives
have been significantly impacted
By the struggles and sacrifices
of our ancestral sages
Our "Rocks in a weary land"
throughout the ages
By performing these rituals
we give praise
To our ancestors as we reaffirm
our African ways.

WHY WE POUR THE LIBATION

Pouring libation in honor of our ancestors
is a very important ritual
An African teaching, an African way,
which has now become an habitual
tradition commencing most of our
ceremonies, commemorations and events
A most meaningful act of dignity,
reverence and eloquence
So not just during the time of Kwanzaa
but during each of the four seasons
Libation is poured to our ancestors
for all of the following reasons.

Libation is poured to our ancestors
to remember and give honor to them;
As a reaffirmation and a verification
of our link to and our life through them;

Libation is poured to our ancestors
To raise before the community
Models of love and struggle,
engagement and service
Of human accomplishment and possibility.

WHY WE POUR THE LIBATION (Continued)

Libation is poured to our ancestors
To express recommitment to the
legacy they saw fit
To bestow upon subsequent generations
By preserving and expanding it

Libation is poured to our ancestors
To cultivate and sustain a cultural practice
Which provides a model for how our children
Should and predictably will act towards us.

In summary, remembrance and honor, posing of
models, recommitment and linkage reaffirmation
Are the reasons why we pay tribute
to our ancestors
By the pouring of the libation.

Remember to never forget.
-AFRICAN   AMERICAN proverb

THE RICHES OF KWANZAA

The riches of Kwanzaa
Are not found in the zawadi
But in the everyday Kwanzaa principles
We embody.

It is not the eye which understands,
but the mind.   -HAUSA proverb

NGUZO SABA (The Seven Principles)

First unity - UMOJA
Unity means we, you and me
Always part of a greater collectivity
A member of a family
A participant in a community
A duplication of a deity
With roots as entrenched as those
of a baobab tree

Second, self-determination - KUJICHAGULIA
The essence of our harambee
The right to determine for myself
What I do and say

Third, UJIMA, collective work and
responsibility
Without which there can be no liberty
We subscribe to the belief that we collectively
Are responsible for our failures and for victories
And commit to the struggle to shape our own destiny.

The fourth principle is UJAMAA -Cooperative
economics
The basis of our prosperity

NGUZO SABA (Continued)

I buy from you and you buy from me
Thereby keeping the money flowing
in our own community
Shared wealth and resources the basis
of African society
The fifth principle is purpose - NIA
And here it is made perfectly clear
That we do not have to go through
life wondering why we are here
Our purpose for being here is to help
Our sisters and our brothers
True greatness never occurs in isolation
But is created in the quality and kinds
of relations we experience with others.

The sixth principle of Kwanzaa is KUUMBA
A self-defining, self-developing
and self-confirming activity
The beauty and benefits we create is
our individual legacy

NGUZO SABA (Continued)

Through creative labor we make a pro-
found and far-reaching contribution to
human history
As doctors, lawyers, engineers, artists...
whoever we choose to be.

Finally, there is faith - IMANI
a belief so strong
It sustains and nourishes us all year long
And enpowers us to hold on

These are the seven values of Kwanzaa
- the Nguzo Saba which reinforce our roots
And aspire us with motivation
to life's higher pursuits.

No matter how high a house is built, it must stand
on something. -EAST AFRICAN proverb

SYMBOLS OF UNITY

During Kwanzaa unity is symbolized by the kikombe
And by the raising of the right arm with open hand
then pulling down and closing that hand into a fist
As we shout "Harambee"

The kikombe cha umoja is first used to pour the
libation
An ancient African tradition; an act of reaffirmation
Then the kikombe cha umoja which is filled with juice
is channeled from hand to hand to lip
With each participant (the wazee first)
taking a symbolic sip.

The fist as a Kwanzaa symbol has historical
significance
First used by Mary McLeod Bethune it too represents
Unity .
During the 1960's it was the "Black Power" symbol
of the African American community.
By having the fingers grouped and working as one
The fist is an energizing image as powerful as the sun.

THE SYMBOLS OF UNITY (Continued)

These two symbols, the kikombe cha umoja
and the fist
Are the unity symbols of Kwanzaa -
which has become a most powerful catalyst
for family development and community building
in African American history
Symbols which represent the first value of
the African American family.

If the fingers of one hand quarrel, they cannot pick
up the food. -EAST AFRICAN proverb

FAMILY

The family must be
The focal point of unity
Not simply siblings, but generations
must be the recipients of
quality human relations.
This means principled and harmonious
living with sisters and brothers
uncles and aunts, fathers and mothers
Relationships based on equality
and reciprocity
Where collective concern and care
Is a family affair.
Where friendship is the fruit
All else is moot.
The family must be
The focal point of unity.

It is hard to fell a tree that is leaning
against a rock. -ASHANTI proverb

KUJICHAGULIA

We must push our own swings
Pull our own strings
Propel our own boats
Save our own throats
Decree
Our own destiny.
Hold a positive vision of what we want
for ourselves and for all humanity
and consistently strive to make
that vision a reality.

Iron won't get hot unless you put it into the
fire.   -CAMEROON proverb

A WILL MADE OF STEEL

A will made of steel
Is a very strong thing
characterized by the mastering
of tenacity, discipline
persistence and domination
An iron-alloyed prerequisite
for self determination
A will made of steel is what
you'll need to possess
To gain the assurance
to experience the success
that comes from designing
your own destiny;
from determining for yourself
what your agenda will be.

The elephant is relevant.
-AFRICAN AMERICAN proverb

GOING THE DISTANCE

Going the distance
No matter how far
If you're truly determined
to be successful
You already are.

Going the distance
Means moving your feet
And persevering during times when
You'd rather retreat.

Going the distance
Means being focused and fit
Means acknowledging and affirming
Your will to commit.

Going the distance
Means chasing your dream
Means doing the things necessary
To nurture your self esteem.

GOING THE DISTANCE (Continued)

Replacing fear with faith
Gives you the strength
To go the distance
To go the length.

Going the distance
No matter how far
If you're truly determined
to be successful
You already are.

The more attempts, the more
successes. -KIKUYU proverb

UJIMA

Ujima at its cultural best
Is an uplifting, progressive communal quest
a collective effort of work and responsibility
of quiet heroism of everyday accountability,.
of kindness and compassion;
charity and consideration
Doing one's share
Living up to social obligations
Beginning with the family
Extending to the community
Our unsung heroes
Promote stability and unity
By being involved to help shape
the various institutions
Which influence our children
They make the real contributions.

If farmers do not cultivate their fields,
the people in the town will die of hunger
-GUINEAN   proverb

UJAMAA

We have not yet recovered
From slavery's economic devastation
Nor have we recovered from
The effects of Jim Crow discrimination
That have perniciously haunted us
Since our emancipation
In spite of expanded opportunities
In employment and education.
Consequently, we continue to be shaped
Not only by slavery's legacy
But by the vestiges of racism
Which hold us back economically.
And by our own attitudes and
Our own buying habits, i.e.,
Our fascinations with designer labels
and electronic gadgetry.
As long as we only invest
In the trappings of success
We will never know true liberty
This must stop. This must end
We must eradicate this trend
Lest our children continue to
inherit only the wind.

You cannot shave a man's head in his absence.
-YORUBA proverb

NIA

Hold your dream in high esteem
Show respect for the goals you set
Feel compelled to excel
Have a mission not just ambition
Keep the faith, hang in there, and commit.

Make purpose and dedication
Your daily aspiration
Give praise for your successes always
Revere that which is dear
Celebrate that which is great
- Yourself and your Kwanzaa holidays.

Anticipate the good so that you may enjoy it.
-ETHIOPIAN   proverb

NIA II

Purpose gives meaning to
whatever we choose to do
Sincerity of purpose combined with faith
Is what will see us through
As we wholeheartedly commit to
Accomplishing our personal best
We will achieve our heart's desire
Our dreams will manifest.

Purpose gives definition to
The tasks we undertake
We enpower ourselves and our purpose
By the choices that we make
The sincerity of our actions and
the intensity of our desires
Is what activates our motivation
Is what ignites our creative fires.

Purpose gives direction
to the path we choose to trek
Our clarity of purpose is what
helps us to select

NIA II (Continued)

The appropriate thoughts needed
to determine the right tack
We know where we're going and
our focus keeps us on track .

Purpose gives significance to our being
to our vision
Available to all by simply
making a committed decision.

The dog has four feet, but he does not walk them
in four roads. -HAITIAN proverb

NIA III

I work wholeheartedly to fulfill my purpose
I refuse to give in to any temptation
Which would cause my creative energy to detour
From my heart's destination.

I do not give in to any weariness
That would negate the completion of what I want to do
An unfinished experience is just not my preference
So I garner the strength to see my purpose through

My vision is clear, always in focus, never distorted
My sincerity of purpose does not allow my goals to be
aborted.

If you follow the elephant you don't have to knock the
dew from the grass. -ASHANTI proverb

KUUMBA

We are a creative people
Behold our pyramids,
Is it any wonder
that our ancient wonder
Is the only one to still stand
A testament to our creative genius
Situated In the heart of the Motherland.

We are a creative people
Out of our Africanness comes
the alphabet, the calendar
the clock, the stethoscope
steel, paper
Our creativity
resonates in our
drums, guitars,
xylophones, banjos,
flutes and harps
our blues, our reggae
our ragtime, our jazz
.
We are a creative people
The original people
Whose creativity flows like the Nile
throughout the universe.

Even when the shield covering wears out
the frame survives.-ASHANTI proverb

PRELUDE

First the drum call
Next the wazee enter
Then a candle is lit
The one in the center
The black candle which
Represents unity
On this first night of Kwanzaa
In the African American community.

DRUM CALL

A CONSTANCY OF FAITH

Enduring imani
eliminates any doubt
Regarding how your life
is going to turn out.

Enduring imani
Is the ammunition
That will propel your dream
To its fruition.

Enduring imani
Precedes your dream's manifestation
For it is your belief that drives your dream
To its successful consummation

What you have seen, you know. What you have
not seen you must believe. -NAMIBIAN proverb

SECURING OUR FUTURE

Securing our future
Is what we do
When we work collectively
To reconstruct and rescue
Our history and our humanity
When we work collectively
To nurture our children,
our vision, our sanity.

A man alone cannot push a dhow
into the sea. KISWAHILI proverb

PRAISESONG

Sing a song of praise
For all the heritage-building ways
We're incorporating the Nguzo Saba
into our essence.
Through collective work and responsibility
Cooperative economics and creativity
We're eternally experiencing
a purposeful presence.

CURTAIN CALL

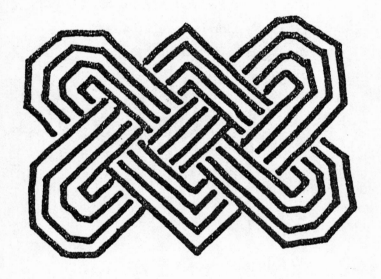

POSTLUDE

Finally, the curtain call
Let us take our bow
And make practicing the
Kwanzaa principles
Our daily vow
We'll end our celebration
Chanting our seven harambee
As we look forward to our future
As we conclude our Kwanzaa holiday.

NGUZO SABA INNUENDOS

Don't expect to promote unity
If you're planning on working alone
Don't expect to express creativity
If you're content to be a clone
Don't expect things to happen
Without taking the initiative
Don't expect to lead a purposeful life
Without learning how to give
Don't expect a sense of direction
To come from without
Don't expect faith to reign
If you're demonstrating doubt.
Don't expect to ever be
All that you can be
If you're unwilling to adopt a
Kawaida philosophy.

If the Earth does not give birth to grass
and grain we die. -SUDANESE proverb

THE INDOMITABLE SPIRIT OF
THE AFRICAN AMERICAN FAMILY

The indomitable spirit
of the African American family

      Is the anthem our babies sing
          emerging from the womb

      Is the determination our warriors wear
          cornrowed into their spines

      Is the resiliency our ancestors hemmorage
          leaping into the light

      Is the drumbeat we inherit
          sirening us to our people's work.

      The indomitable spirit
          of the African American family

Is the poetry of our third eye.

The son of an elephant will never be a dwarf.
-YORUBA   proverb

KWANZAA CANDLE POWER

Out of the abyss of uncertainty
My soul begins to tower
As my faith is rekindled
by Kwanzaa candle power

It is a growing light
Shining bright
Shining brighter every hour
Kwanzaa candle power

It is an illuminated seed
Addressing a need
A blossoming flower
Kwanzaa candle power

Lack of knowledge is darker than night.
-HAUSA proverb

KWANZAA KWAHERI

Strive for discipline, dedication and
achievement in all that you do
Dare struggle and sacrifice and
gain the strength that will come to you
Build where you are and dare leave
a legacy that will remain
For as long as the sun shines;
For as long as the clouds rain.

Practice daily the Nguzo Saba
Umoja,   Kujichagulia
Ujima, Ujamaa, Kuumba,
Imani and Nia
And may the wisdom of our ancestors
reside within you and me
As we commit daily to our values -
-values of the African American family.

May the year's end meet us laughing
and stronger than the year before

KWANZAA KWAHERI (Continued)

May our children honor us
by following our example
of love and labor forever more

And at the end of next year, may we sit again
together as a nation
With greater achievement and a higher level
of human life and closer to liberation.

Cultivation will never cease.
-KIKUYU   proverb

CALL TO UNITY

When we do our call to unity
This is what we say

Harambee
Harambee
     Harambee
     Harambee
          Harambee
          Harambee
               Harambee!

This one word phrase "Harambee"
Means "Let us pull together"
A Kiswahili chant uttered
To unite a people forever.

We say harambee seven times
To honor and reinforce
The Nguzo Saba
-Values of the African American family,
Of course.

Let the singers sing in unison, then the
job can be done. -ZULU proverb

JohnnieRenee Nelson lives in San Diego, CA with her husband and their three children. She is a member of the African American Writers and Artists, Inc. of San Diego and California Poets in the Schools and has been involved with numerous programs in the area. While completing her graduate studies Ms. Nelson earned the coveted Michigan State University Creative Writing Award for Best Collection of Poetry for her first volume, "21 Years Toward Becoming a Black Woman". A Quest for Kwanzaa, Ms. Nelson's second volume of poetry was heralded as the authoratative genesis of Kwanzaa literature. Ms. Nelson has traveled extensively throughout Africa, Europe, Canada and the Caribbean and is currently completing two works in progress, BLACK BEAUTY: POEMS ABOUT OUR PEOPLE and WHEN KWANZAA COMES: A CHILD'S FIRST BOOK OF KWANZAA POEMS.